Where Do Hearts Grow?

A Little Book of Hidden Hearts

Debi Novotny

To my parents, Joe, Joenne, Jim, and Lorraine
For all the love they've given me.
 D.N.

Where Do Hearts Grow?
A Little Book of Hidden Hearts, 1st edition

Text Copyright@ 2020 by Debi Novotny

All Rights Reserved

No part of this publication may be reproduced, stored in a retrieval system or transmitted in any form by any means electronic, mechanical, or photocopying, recording or otherwise without the permission of the author.

Library of Congress Control Number: 2020909736

ISBN: 978-1-7337457-0-3

A very special thank you goes to Sandy Wicks for the breathtaking maple tree heart picture and to Asher Fox for the beautiful Gilded Flicker bird feather picture. More thanks to Phoebe Fox, Maria Lanigan, Deb Breeze, Maria Messenger, and Barbara Renner for sending me their amazing heart pictures! Heartfelt thanks to a dynamic editing crew: Gwen, Jamie, Kellie, Jim, Phoebe, Barbara, and Pat!

Sooner or later, we all cross the path of a heart.

The best kind of heart is hidden until found, but where do hearts grow? Let's find out!

Can you guess where this spiky heart grew?

It grew on a prickly pear cactus pad found in the desert.

Fun Fact
The Sonoran Desert is one of the hottest deserts of the United States, reaching temperatures of 118°F. It is home to the prickly pear cactus and many animals including roadrunners, javelinas, and rattlesnakes.

Can you guess where this fuzzy heart grew?

It grew on the back of a black and white puppy.

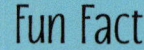

Fun Fact
A puppy is a young dog. It is a furry, four-legged, tail wagging animal that loves to run and play! Their fur grows in a variety of colors and patterns.

Can you guess where this green heart grew?

It grew from a pickled cucumber found squished inside a pickle jar.

Fun Fact
A pickle is a cucumber that has been soaked in salty water. You can find cucumbers growing in most vegetable gardens.

Can you guess where this mini heart grew?

It grew inside a juicy ripe watermelon.

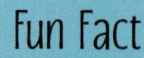

Fun Fact
Refreshing watermelons are both a fruit and a vegetable. They are called watermelons because they're mostly made up of water!

Can you guess where this blue heart grew?

It grew on the colorful tail feather of a peacock.

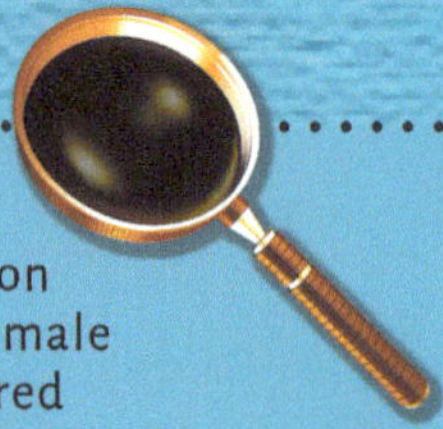

Fun Fact
Peacocks are one of the largest flying birds on earth. The male bird is called a peacock, the female is named a peahen, and the babies are referred to as peachicks. The male peacock feathers are called a train, and he sheds it every year.

Can you guess where this brown heart grew?

It grew near the branch of a favorite shade tree.

Fun Fact
A shade tree in the desert is a welcome resting spot for animals looking for relief from the hot sun. Shade trees come in all shapes and sizes!

Can you guess where this whole heart grew?

It grew way up high on a majestic canyon wall.

Fun Fact
Canyon de Chelly National Monument is located in Northeastern Arizona. The name means "rock canyons". Navajo families make their homes here and farm the land in the canyon. Can you see the petroglyphs on the canyon wall?

Can you guess where these tiny hearts grew?

They grew on the feathers of a Gilded Flicker bird.

Fun Fact
The Gilded Ficker bird grows feathers with tiny hearts on them. This male bird made his nest in a saguaro cactus.

Can you guess where this bumpy heart grew?

It grew on the bark of a tall pine tree.

Fun Fact
Tall pine trees grow in the forest. The outer bark of a pine tree is the thick, scaly covering that protects it from cold, heat, and insects.

Can you guess where this rocky heart grew?

It grew near shells and pebbles on a sandy beach.

Fun Fact
Along the seashore on the beach, a heart rock was found surrounded by seashells, pebbles, and sand. A beach lies along the edge of an ocean, lake, or river.

Can you guess where these two hearts grew?

They grew on the trunk of a wise old tree.

Fun Fact
A wise old tree eventually becomes a shelter for small animals, insects, and reptiles. They make homes in the branches and tree trunk to stay safe from predators.

Can you guess where this wooden heart grew?

It grew inside a 130 year old maple tree.

Fun Fact
This soft maple tree grew for generations on a farm in Iowa. It started as a young sapling and reached its full height of 65 feet tall when it turned 130 years old. The tree was often tapped for sweet maple syrup and its leaves turned red and orange in the fall.

Do you know where else
a heart grows?

A special heart grows in you!

Where have you found a heart?

Glue your own picture here

We'd love to see where you find little hidden hearts!
#wheredoheartsgrow

www.ingramcontent.com/pod-product-compliance
Lightning Source LLC
Chambersburg PA
CBHW042250100526
44587CB00002B/91